Always a Groomsman and Never the Groom

by

Steven Fitzgerald Gooden-Champ

Published by

Steven F. Gooden-Champ
P.O. Box 5313
Orange, CA 92863 USA

ISBN: 1-460901-93-2

ISBN-13: 978-1-460901-93-9

Library of Congress Control Number: 2011904267

Printed in the United States of America

Dedication

To the end that a dedication bestows special attention to but a few, it would be easier for me to dedicate to no one, for there are so many to which I desire to dedicate this literary effort. However, being that there is no greater gift than that of a child, I am bound with the deepest gratitude to G-d for having given me a son. I dedicate the best of what I was able to achieve, notwithstanding my flaws, to Oner, my son, the most exquisite one of all.

Contents

Acknowledgments

I would like to acknowledge the inspiring and tireless efforts of my son, Reno-Oner, for his countless contributions in helping me fine-tune the broad brushstrokes of my vision. I also wish to thank Carl Nagy, Karl Lofgren, and the Welter and Tarpley families for their humble and generous assistance and guidance in the professional editing of this book.

Foreword

"Always a groomsman and never the groom" at first glance sounds like a sister phrase to "always a bridesmaid and never the bride," an adage that usually evokes a sad dissertation about a woman who can't seem to find a husband, or is getting up in years and still unmarried. Men are never referred to with this sort of demeaning verbiage. Rarely are we frowned upon for delaying marriage or waiting later in life to marry (if at all). But for women it is a foregone conclusion that a finger without a wedding ring is like a bird without wings, a caterpillar that never transforms into a butterfly. The unmarried woman is marked, and that mark is a capital "S" for "Still Single" a scarlet letter of disgrace.

"Always a Groomsman and Never the Groom" is a noble celebration of men who groom one another as mentors or advisors. We refer to these men as "a man's man," a strong motivator, an encourager, and a compassionate individual. These days it is rare to find men such as this, who dedicate their lives expressly to the success of others. The stories in this book are about men that man up, step up and rise up, achieving their highest and best.

Specifically this book is my personal oblation to G-d, and a declaration of a call to groom my fellow man. Awakening the lion within each man or kicking the mule within him is a noble task to perform. I've learned to see the humor when applying a swift kick to the posterior of the mule within a man; it's often the kick that gets us going. I've learned the value of offering wise counsel: approaching the lion with caution, waking him up, and reminding him of his duty. Having been kicked many times, I have learned the value of being roused out of my lion's den. In all honesty, it is this process of kicking and awakening that if continued, makes us all better men.

In today's world, sister tides of complacency and mediocrity wash away our every effort to demand or expect more of each other and ourselves. Rarely seen is any open display of masculinity, as our society has been transformed into a feminist enclave of political correctness. Many men have abdicated their paternal duties, as well as their marital responsibilities. While pushing the family off the cliffs of life, we watch as they spin in a free fall, plunging to a precipitous demise.

1

The Big Game

The Big Game has started and the pass has been thrown: the receiver is at the 20 yard line, the 30 yard line, the 40, and at the 45 yard line he fumbles the ball - it's a turnover. The men are left standing, watching their lost possession now carried down the stretch in the opposite direction in the hands of the women. Left now on the sidelines or out of the stadium entirely, the men watch in shame and disgrace as the game of life is played out in a demoralizing fashion, right in front of them.

Today's feminization of the masculine is heralded as an improvement of traditional gender roles, "power sharing correctness" as some may call it. While the feminine have taken on the masculine with all its worst traits in the name of equality, the masculine have taken on the feminine traits, in pursuit of lasciviousness. Role reversal and gender confusion has created a maze of perplexities in gender relations. The intellectual modernist lounges around pontificating questions like, "What's a man or a family?" "What's right or wrong?" What was once considered common sense is in today's halls of academia considered mysteries of the universe.

Since its inception, this cultural erosion has left us with little moral shore to stand on. The erosion of foundational truths has overridden many of our traditional institutions. The enchanting and seducing songs of the "Sirens" call to us, with the sole intent to destroy us. The modernist's ideas and philosophies race toward us like a tsunami, wiping away all semblance of honor, courage and integrity. Now, a series of moral-less waves pounds us into submission, drowning us under its decrees and commands. We struggle to rise to the surface for air, only to be forced under by a continual swell, one after another. Finally, we rise, only to find a new reality afloat.

Who is left, that will hear the call and respond to this catastrophe? Which of us will stand up and confront this enemy with the weaponry of righteousness: ideas, beliefs and actions whose time has come?

For myself, I have been called to search out men stranded by this disastrous event and rescue them from the cultural rip tides that drag them out into the sea of conformity. Teaching men to resist the pride that beckons them to swim where they should not is in itself challenging. Succumbing to ego, while being force-fed by their culture, redefines them and lures them into a cave of hibernation. Consequently, they are drained of their strength in the struggle to resist, and are inevitably overwhelmed by demagoguery and their own apathy.

Let's ask ourselves these questions: Was it naiveté that did them in? Pride, fear or just a lack of training for their mission? "Hind sight" is as they say, and yet unfortunately for us, too many times ignored in our own choices. Like the cycles of the equinox we repeat our mistakes with impeccable precision, never learning from our history, and thus repeating it.

Now filled with a life of regrets, of would'ves, could'ves and should'ves, we are tormented in our sleep with nightmares of dreams never followed and visions never brought to life. These unfulfilled dreams and visions do not make a future for our sons.

In the stables of our homes, where this grooming takes shape, is the best remedy for our sons. There they are equipped and prepared for the race on the winding tracks of life. In our homes (our grooming stables), we learn the habits, practices and maneuvers needed to get through life. Our fathers and mothers teach us how to properly navigate both expected and unexpected curves, drops, bumps and dips. They teach us how to read the signs that point us in the right direction, and demonstrate to us when to take the detours that help us avoid the unseen dangers. We learn in the home how to use sound discernment and make good judgments. Following these methods will help guide us steadily on our path and teach us to change direction when needed.

Rebuilding and restoring the moral foundations beneath our feet provides the ground needed to regain our footing. We must stem the tide of these moral-less waves that are vanquishing the honor of our men. We must prevent the lowering of standards we once held high. As mentors, fathers and spiritual advisors, we should endeavor to work towards the goal of breathing new life into our standard bearers, our sons. We should set new benchmarks and hallmarks of justice, mercy and grace, providing a conduit to good conduct that is without obstruction. Finally we who teach and preach these things must, and should, live in such a way that those watching will want to follow after our example. Let's give this world something to reach for, strive for, something beyond what they believe is possible, enabling them to do the impossible. Too long we've applauded those who have given so little, that when one gives so much, we think it's too much.

Shore up the foundations that have been battered and worn, weakened by both time and tumult. Begin building a noble legacy, worthy of a generation's best accomplishments, and pass it on. Let's repair the breaches in the walls that have been broken down. Light the way to the path that sets men in the right direction. Build a bulwark for our children's future and a rampart for their posterity. Start grooming our cubs and tangle-haired lions again. Remaining faithful in these principles will guarantee for our sons the tools needed and the knowledge of how to use them for their generation's challenges. Dark clouds of a perverse generation's ideology continue to billow on the horizon. Inching towards us, they are anxious to drench us with their acid rain of conformity. Be a counter storm of your own, answering with a torrential downpour of integrity and righteousness.

Now is the time, gentleman, to start your engines! Get out your groom brooms and sweep - it's time to groom! Always the groomsman for some, and one day the groom for others. GROOOOOOOOOOOOOM!

2

The Groom

Oddly enough the term "groom" by definition refers to the grooming and care of horses or can be applied to any animal in a stable. It might appear to be an insult to refer to a man as a groomsman when applying the real definition of the term. However, after a closer examination, it's both meaningful and complimentary. For decades the opposite gender (female) has often referred to men using animal connotations (e.g., dogs). Well, now they can add "horse" to that infamous list.

Etymologically speaking, the word "Groomsman" means "To clean horses, or one who tends to, manicures and generally cares for them." To remove dirt, parasites, fur or feathers

---

What does the word "Groom" mean?

- qualify, dispose
- cleanse, clean
- shave
- comb, comb out, disentangle
- dress, arrange, set, do, coif, coiffure
- mousse, gel
- pomade
- clean up
- make up
- manicure
- barber
- pedicure
- doll up, do up, pretty up, glam up
- spruce up, spruce, slick up
- smarten up
- perfume, scent

---

from the skin of an animal was the primary duty of a groomsman. This brings new meaning to the role of groomsmen and gives ladies way too much ammunition for their verbal assaults.

Remember when you were just a boy, hearing your mother's voice, calling for you to get cleaned up and ready for dinner. Whether it was logging off the computer, getting off the basketball court, out of the water, or down from a tree, it was the call to groom that told us dinner was ready. Surely we can admit to hearing the all too familiar grooming calls for other purposes, like the call to shower and get dressed for church, mass, or Shabbat. What about Monday Morning School or that famously renowned rise before dawn for that paper route. Then there's the call for brushing our teeth before bed, changing into our pajamas, combing our hair before the relatives arrive or zipping up that permanently stuck zipper. How many times do you recall being told to tie your shoelaces or wipe that snotty nose? Pony up guys (heee haaw)! I know all of this sounds quite familiar. Most of us continue these practices of our childhood grooming well into our adult lives. The rituals, habits and routines we grew up with carry over into our first interview, our first day on the job, even our first date.

Searching out the right tie, shoes, socks and jacket seemed to take forever. Primping in the mirror to get the hair perfect, the teeth white, and the breath fresh ... ahhhhh. According to anthropologists even early man groomed himself and the others in his tribe. Zoologists also inform us of the animal kingdoms proclivity to groom (e.g., crows, monkeys, dogs and cats).

Understanding the power of first impressions is one of the most important principles of Grooming. The age-old adage "don't judge a book by its cover" seems to contradict the principles of grooming. After all, why not judge a book by its cover; seeing that before one can read a book, there is only the cover to judge it by. It is after all, what we first see.

In dating we base our initial "cover judgments" on sheer looks, determining if we want to ask a girl out or not, knowing nothing really about her. We buy clothes based on how they look in the store, only to return them after having changed our minds at home. We buy food, based on how appealing it is or on the style of its packaging. We do this by making an aesthetic judgment. More often than not we are dissatisfied with the choices we've made; choices made simply from an initial judgment. What was the last movie you saw? Did you see it based on a cover judgment (e.g., a trailer or review)? Were you surprised at how different it was from the trailer that lured you in? Was it better or worse than you initially thought? The point is, we do judge many things by their cover, and that is normal. What we must emphasize is the importance of continuing to judge more deeply. Always re-assess and re-evaluate in order to validate or invalidate what you first believed to be true. The layers of judgment are a textbook outline of "Observation 101." They are sight, sound, smell, taste, and touch. These sensory layers serve to assist us in making the best judgments we can. I hope you apply this approach when reading this book. The cover's implied message is reflected in the stories told and principles outlined.

3

The Groomsmen

A groomsman is one of the male attendants to the bridegroom. He selects his closest friends and/or relatives to serve in this capacity; it is an honor to be selected. From the groomsmen the groom chooses his best man. The duties are to help guests find their places and to participate in the wedding ceremony. Planning celebratory events such as a <u>bachelor party</u>, or providing help with gifts, luggage and any unexpected need that may come up. One of the most comical traditions is the desecration of sorts of the "Wedding Car" - a humorous, sentimental gesture of affection and bon voyage to newlyweds, without the often embarrassing commentary scribbled all over the windows.

In a military officer's wedding, swordsmen of the <u>honor guard</u> replace the role of groomsmen. They are usually picked as close personal friends of the groom who have served with him. How fitting they are called "Honor Guard!"

Best man is the head male assistant to the bridegroom at a wedding. In our Western culture, the groom extends this honor to someone who is close to him: a father, brother or close friend.

In the past, the bachelor party was typically scheduled for a convenient evening during the week before the wedding. A type of farewell dinner, it's paid for and sponsored by the bridegroom, but it can also be fully organized and paid for by the groom's friends.

In <u>Eastern Orthodox</u> weddings in <u>Greece</u>, the best man is often also the <u>koumbaros</u> or religious sponsor, and is traditionally the groom's godfather.

In the <u>Ukraine</u> a best man's job is guarding the bride. When he or the groom steps away, the bride gets "kidnapped" or has a shoe stolen. Then the groom or the best man must pay a <u>ransom</u> in exchange for returning the bride, usually by paying money (which is given to the bride) or by doing something embarrassing. In western cultures we do what's known as the "Money Dance" where the best man collects the money from wedding patrons that wish to dance with either the groom or the bride.

In the African country of <u>Uganda</u> a best man is expected to guide the newlyweds in the ways of marriage. This means that ideally a best man must be married, preferably to one wife, and should be in position to give sound, tried and tested advice. A best man must be a <u>confidant</u> and be discreet in the details he shares about marriage.

In <u>Bhutan</u> the best man is the official ceremonial guardian to both bride and groom. He entertains the guests, sometimes for several hours, keeping the celebration going.

We rename terms constantly, taking them in and out, back and forth from their original meaning. Redefining them entirely based on pop, political, ideological and technological changes in our culture. This can be a good thing, but more often than not it is a bad thing.

4

Horsing Around

<u>Stud</u>: A virile, capable male horse for reproduction purposes.

When applied to men, it refers to one in good physical condition and able to father healthy children. These are the ones most sought after for breeding or mating. (Just ask a horse breeder.)

<u>Donkey</u>: Ass of the Horse family, never looked upon as romantically as the horse.

However, looking closer at this less than aesthetically appealing animal, it's not the stubborn quality that it should be famous for. The Donkey or Ass is actually quite the dependable beast, versatile in function. When travelling long distances it is more graceful, able to endure and navigate treacherous mountain terrain. The Donkey was the primary animal used in ancient farming, dating back to the Phoenician and Egyptian empires. The donkey is a capable beast of burden, used in farming and in transportation of goods. Unlike the horse, donkeys never throw off their riders. In fact, even prospectors realized their dependable, reliable behavior. They could trust a donkey to NOT obey an accidental or erroneous command to turn and step off a cliff ledge. Horses would sometimes unthinkingly obey, with tragic results.

Hebrew prophets (Samuel, Elijah, Elisha), kings (Saul, David, Solomon), and even Mary and Jesus were famous for riding them. Looks like the donkey has some pretty good references. Perhaps stubborn should be replaced with determined, dependable, focused and able.

Is it not amazing that the Groom, the "Horse of a man," has a calling that the very title (groom) encompasses. That calling is to be the donkey, and navigate the difficult terrain of life with grace, carrying burdens responsibly. There is nothing like an occasional swift kick-in-the-ass to the Ass, when he grows tired and restless, to get him going again. After all, the military has been kicking our son's (donkeys) asses for decades. Fathers send their sons in as stubborn little asses and the military sends them back as willing noble stallions, willing to take on any dare and duty, face death and stare it down, climb any terrain and run any race. These are the attributes of a man who has had good stable training, good cleaning and a good kick-in-the-ass (excuse the pun).

5

Men Are Horses, Women Are Their Riders?

One author wrote "Men are from Mars - Women are from Venus," but I think a better comparison is a combination of a horse and an ass to describe our traits. Better said is perhaps something like, "Men are sometimes Horses, sometimes Asses, and Women are their Riders." Either way, horse or ass, be a noble one. Be versatile in your contribution to your fellow man, run with fervor and power like the Horse, the race set before you, and be productive and fruitful like the stallion-stud. However like the Ass (donkey) carry your bride through the bumps along the road and trials of life, with grace and faithfulness. Bear your burden and responsibilities well, and with joy.

All this being said, the terms groom, groomsman and best man all have quite colorful origins. If we reflect in our actions the names and titles that we bear, we might fare better in our quest to become our highest and best.

How fitting these terms are for men, like iron sharpening iron. We do this for one another, presenting ourselves as men created in the image of G-d and ultimately made suitable for the Bride.

As we began life, birthed out of the gate of the wombs of our mothers, screaming and in shock, hating baths, hating being cleaned from all orifices (i.e., noses, ears, eyes and the rest), so it is as we begin our own grooming of character. It wasn't too long ago when we found ourselves getting through those terrible 2's and then that first dreadful haircut. How I recall that first time in a barber's chair at the Barbershop. Boy, did I squirm while being held down as they cut and trimmed me to my parents delight. We do need to be groomed by others through our life, and can eventually grow accustomed to being groomed or grooming ourselves with a degree of accuracy. Funny, as we grow older, we pay to have others groom us (some paying too much), and enjoy it. Then we mature to the point where we willingly allow ourselves to be groomed.

Gentlemen, our future Brides are in the stands of life waiting for the race to commence, cheering us on, I pray. Let's storm out the gates hitting the track running, making them gasp in awe of our strength, majesty, character and stature. We are groomed, groomers, grooming and ultimately the GROOM.

Welcoming the Professional groomers to help us with the dirt in our lives, the parasites and feathers that have attached themselves to us can only make us better. Sit back, relax, and allow your feet to be washed, hair shampooed, and skin scrubbed down. Keep good mirrors in your life, and keep them clean, so you always have a reference point reflecting and reminding you without distortion of your true self. Those mirrors are your own honesty, friends that speak sincerely to you, and an occasional unbiased third party opinion. Set a righteous standard that is higher than your own measure. Give yourself something to reach for, live and walk in spiritual truth, respecting the rule of law. Though many debate it, there is no denying that there exists an unwritten law and moral code for all humanity. It's the G-d conscience and it is inalienable. Remember these rules and meditate upon them, they will teach you, guide you, groom and prepare you. This is the groomsman, the best man, the GROOM, and I am "Always a Groomsman and Never the Groom."

6

To Marry or Not To Marry...

The men that groom us, besides our immediate family, may be men from our community, businesses or places of worship. They can be public figures, celebrities, professionals, athletes, pastors, police, politicians, firemen, carpenters or ditch diggers. It makes no difference the occupation, the race, color, creed, or class of man. If the groom is an honorable man he will look for honorable like-minded men to stand with him - men who reflect his worldview in some areas, yet differ in others, however still sharing a common respect for his core values and principles. It can be the groomsman who first recognizes in a friend or family member the potential of a man ready to become the groom. It is this scenario, of the groomsman identifying a man to become a groom that you will see played out in the stories told in this book.

We are bombarded from childhood with the expectations or dreams of marrying and starting a family. It's our unspoken genetic programming, an innate expectation of our purpose. Nowhere is this more personified than in the lives of our daughters and sisters. This rule is, to some, like an albatross around their necks, more a burden to them than a blessing. But to most, it is a joyful pursuit. Every woman desperate to marry and have kids feels this pressure, and waits or seeks for a proper suitor to be found. If she finds none, the scourge begins and she is called an "old maid" or worse. There has to be a proper candidate, one of the "male" order, and that means a Jock, dude, a guy, a man. These are just a few of the titles given for a groom-to-be. Some refer to us as dogs, players, jerks, losers, useless, pimps and scumbags. These of course are terms used by the cynical. Explaining or defending these derogatory terms, justified or not, is best left for another day. What I will do is emphasize the proper names and definitions we as groomsmen and grooms should bear. Names that our sons, fathers, brothers, and friends reflect should be names with a reputation of honor, integrity, character, and morality.

Marriage is honorable, the very pillar and foundation of a civilized society. It is the primary method by which the glue of community is formed, the bond of tribes, nations and governments. We are all made up of one social thread of humanity - family! It is here where we first learn the social tools of diplomatic cooperation and both individual and community responsibility. Here is where the lines are drawn, while others are decisively and defiantly crossed.

Without marriages (one of the oldest institutions of man) our society would utterly collapse upon itself. We need marriages, men and women making families, forming covenants and fulfilling vows. In our modern world, families are defined as same-sex couples or people living together having babies and this is ever increasing. We are desperate for men to model a better way, recapturing our traditions that embody timeless and formidable truths. We need a revival of etiquette, manners, class and decency, regaining a sense of common values.

Some will not marry - why? Some will remain single for life, or for the majority of their life. There is a purpose in singleness, let there be no doubt about that. But that being said, singleness ultimately serves the institution of marriage, directly or indirectly, much like an Oscar-winning film in which an actor gets an award for a supporting role.

Unlike women who end up ostracized and treated like a cast-off when not married, men in many instances are seen as playboys - virile, sexually alluring, and ladies' men. Terms like "Mac-daddy," "pimp," and "cool" are revered as endearing for men such as these. This societal perspective is not one to which I subscribe. Perhaps better yet, others see these men as non-committal, irresponsible, juvenile, refusing to grow up and take on true responsibility. Any combination of the above can reflect a lack of true character in a man. Some however remain single due to sexual confusion, abuse (sexual or mental trauma) and/or homosexuality. Some or all of these can explain the man who remains unmarried. This book however will focus on yet another premise I consider the perennial cause of non-marrying men. The lack of grooming men to be grooms, and the absence of fathers with right teachings, is the primary cause for our current state of manhood.

The clarion call to be a groomer of men for men's sake, if followed, will rescue the wayward man from a vow-less abyss, ultimately leading him down the path towards holy matrimony.

For the wayward man who is incapable, unqualified, or just unmotivated, the groomsman is his centaur, his drill sergeant, and his kick-in-the-ass to get things jump-started. For the angry, unforgiving, victimized and haughty man, the groomsman can be his center, reminding him to return to the basics of who he is. For the steady, solid, consistent, strong and humble man, the groomsman is his brother in arms, comrade, co-worker and affirmer of what already is, encouraging him to stay the course and persevere. The role of the groomsman is to help prepare the groom for his wedding day, strengthening him when he is weak, re-focusing him when he drifts off course, leading him when he lags, and lifting him up when he falls. The groomsman watches his back, speaks to him honestly, and is faithful to a fault. He is dependable, loving as a brother, and like an archer, keeps his eye on the target, aiming for the bull's eye, the prize of the bride. He helps, but never enables, leads but never recklessly, advises but never too quickly. He is always seeking what is in the best interest of the groom.

The groomsman never cowers, isn't envious or jealous, and sacrifices his own interests to benefit that of the groom's. His joy is seeking his friend's steady growth, while helping avoid the pitfalls and detours that can delay or altogether prevent his becoming the best that he can.

Although each man may be different in one way or another, the groomsman remains the same. Simply put he is constant, reliable and ready to serve. Above all he is that "friend that loves at all times" that "sticks closer than a brother." Some groomsmen are appointed only for the occasion or the ceremony, and yet others are "Groomsman for Life." Those groomsmen who are married men are best suited to dispensing discreet advice to the newly wed. He can assist the new groom in identifying the obstacles, while devising a plan for overcoming them. His counsel is invaluable to the new groom, as he prepares him for his marital journey. In the Ugandan tradition, the father of the groom typically plays this role, and by all accounts, he is the most important of all the groomsmen.

No greater love can I find, than that of a father for his sons and daughters. Our world's history is filled with stories of fathers and sons, side by side in battles, victories or defeats. At times they are at odds with each other over expectations. However, no matter how good or bad, it is evident that the father's role plays the most significant and impressionable part in grooming. The father is the engine that drives his sons to failure, or the rocket that propels them to unimaginable heights and achievements.

The father groomsman can be the biological father or not. The more important factor of this role is that the man, whoever he might be, is a father in spirit. The life experiences of the father form a syllabus of sorts for the groom-to-be. This syllabus provides for him a head start, improving his prospects of survival, and reinforcing truths taught and lessons learned. When put into practice, it will give him a platform from which to launch future generations.

Most men, in our Romanized western culture, are missing fathers or father figures. In fact most fathers themselves have vacated their paternal duties and responsibilities, leaving their children to be preyed upon by a mindless pack-styled society of wolves and coyotes. The absence of fathers, or even the presence of bad ones, causes our sons to grow up resembling well-groomed monkeys rather than tangle-haired lions.

Personally, I would rather resemble a rough-looking lion than a smoothly primped monkey.

Grooming our sons starts at birth, but can begin much later. In any case, it should begin and continue until that man is ready, prepared, or equipped to assume his role. Few of us will have the perfect scenario, although it exists. The path of least resistance always lures us away from the one of greater effort. Obtaining our goals, quicker and with greater ease is the modern world's motto. We prefer to virtually connect with everything, even our own thoughts and heart's desires via altered reality. Preferring to text rather than saying it face to face, demonstrates our true lack of inter-communication skills. We label this "a safe way to meet and greet," while actually ending up knowing less about the person because we see only what the technology reveals to us. We hide behind these technological toys (iPods, cell-phones, computers, social-networking sites) claiming connectivity, while ever widening the chasm of disconnect with every technological advance.

Someone once asked me, "How do we groom a man in this groom-less world of endless pursuit of the aesthetic, the facade, the superficial?" How do we take back the reins of the rules of grooming, rules men once lived and died by? We change this only by starting fresh, with a new generation. What's lost is lost, but what once was great can be great again, and can again be our crown of glory.

New wine can't be put in old wineskins lest they burst. We need new wineskins, a new generation to pour the wine of grooming into. When that happens we will be ready to step into our roles and go beyond our fathers' mediocrity, fulfilling our duty and taking our place, alongside our brides and our children.

Lambs to Lions

Fathers Rise! And rise again!
Sons into boys,
Boys into young men,
Young men into men, and
Men into grooms, like
Lambs to lions.

There is a groomsman for every groom and whoever that may be, he will be the man that sleeps with integrity, fights with honor, lives by character and dies leaving a legacy. He knows who he is, and where he is going, while always reminding himself of his duty. The groomsman himself was a man once groomed; he sat at the feet of a greater teacher. He has learned diligently, endured faithfully and groomed consistently, while keeping himself from the grip of his vices. Now he teaches and seeks out others willing to learn and to be groomed - those who can follow humbly, listen intently and act passionately. He seeks men who thirst for honor, and hunger for integrity. To these men will belong the crown of the groom, the jewel which is the Bride.

The following chapters will tell best the methods, means and madness of my techniques in grooming grooms. This is my story a lopsided dedication of singleness in the salvation of men, who ultimately become grooms. The call to become the groom rests within the caldron of the heart of every man. These stories are true, sad and comedic, but all with one goal in mind, grooming grooms. These stories are my own, not borrowed or manufactured, but lived out in tears and joy. Peer in, take a peek and contemplate the tales of the man who is "Always a Groomsman and Never the Groom."

7
Groom 1 – The Yacht

There I stood, keeper of the ring, the symbol of a promise, a vow he had made to his bride-to-be. No small matter to have been chosen, picked out of a cluster of friends, family and acquaintances to stand with him on his wedding day. The groomsman's role itself is a meaningful, deliberate call; he plays a role in the groom's mental, physical and spiritual growth. He is a man the groom may have cried with, laughed with, played all the games in life that men and boys play. He may have been involved with the groom in business, or simply may have been there for him at a crucial moment. He may have known him his whole life, or only more recently. Nonetheless he is significant to the groom, and holds a unique spot in the groom's heart.

The groomsman is the ultimate man's man, so as the best man, there I stood even more highly honored, chosen above the others to be "Keeper of the Ring," the symbol of covenant and promise to his bride. This is a time-cherished tradition that no groomsman or best man should ever take for granted.

Understanding my role fills me (the groomsman, the best man) with humility and pride, and simply put, with unspeakable joy. Being chosen is one thing, but willingly accepting the offer to stand with him is still my choice, which brings me to the point of this book. It isn't being chosen to stand with the groom on his wedding day that qualifies me as a groomsman, anymore than standing with the bride makes him truly a "Groom." That happens long before the wedding day, long before the bachelor party, before he asks you to be a groomsman, or his very own engagement. It begins at the moment of birth, at the moment a family is formed and a father begins to pour into his children. It continues when men begin to interact with other men in their social groups. It is in these social clusters where men begin to form friendships that can produce familial bonds. Many bonds form during early childhood, college years, or thereafter. One thing is certain, at some point it must commence, and hopefully before you're married. Nothing's scarier to a bride than realizing her groom has to learn to be a man on her watch.

There we both stood on the deck of the Yacht. The skies were blue, the ocean calm. The sun glistened off the water as it beamed down on beads of sweat congregating like a crowd upon my head. It's another typical sunny day in Orange County, but actually not so typical, for this was the wedding day of my friend, my first groom who had picked me as Best Man, Craig. I was the keeper of the ring. We had devised a plan to dangle the wedding ring precariously at the end of a fishing line, with the pole perched against the railing on the bow of the ship. You can just imagine all the possible outcomes of this plan...let's not!

The moment had arrived and I was nudged for the ring, all eyes turned towards me, the best man. I patted my pockets and jacket and hunched my shoulders in confusion. My eyes darted about and the audience gasped nervously while piercing me with their gaze. I jetted around the other groomsmen, hurried to the bow of the ship, and reeled in the line. There ... the ring at the end. AHHHHHH. The crowd sighed in relief, along with the bride, as I passed the "Precious" (the Ring) to the groom. Smiles and laughs ensued as the tension subsided. All was well, and my inaugural turn at best man went off without a hitch. We had managed the ultimate, successful, unexpected surprise without a glitch. It was absolutely flawless. Perhaps this is a precursor to all such future wedding events ... not! Craig was now a Married Man!

During the reception, I took time to reflect on all the events that led up to that day. I recalled the first day I met Craig, how we became friends, and brothers united by a shared faith in our Lord Jesus. We became trusted confidants to one another. We shared many memorable occasions together, from my first surf session in Corona Del Mar, to my first ride on dirt bikes (Yamaha 125 & 250 expert series). He was a bit of a daredevil, Craig. His father was a good man, a hard worker and a loving parent. His father demonstrated leadership and a loving discipline, something I had not grown up seeing. I knew early in our friendship that my views and opinions mattered to Craig, and that weighed heavily upon me. I was careful with my words, and guarded my thoughts, deliberately keeping them to myself at times, while generously dispensing them (like an overflowing dam) at other times. As the years progressed, my friend eventually found a love interest. In many ways she seemed much like him, adventurous in sport and excited about life. I encouraged him to pray for direction with regard to the role she could play as a future wife. Over time and after some prayerful consideration, it had become obvious that G-d would allow this union and it wasn't long after they were married. To this day they remain married and in love, my first round as best man was now behind me.

8

The Journey

The satisfaction you get from mentoring men (sons, brothers, and friends) and watching them take the next step and graduate to the class of "The Married," is a tremendous feeling of accomplishment. Watching men mature and take on their respective roles is humbling. It strengthens our resolve to continue. After standing with Craig on his wedding day, I wanted from that moment on to stand with others and play that role in other men's lives. I wanted to be a man's man, a groomsman.

Saving a dying society can be a reality, if we put our brothers, friends and sons above all selfish ambition and mindless dreams. There is no limit to what men who are singularly focused can achieve. For now the world has one more groom from the ranks of the single ones, willingly changing the world by his one act of sacred matrimony, his oblation to G-d.

California is a land flowing with milk and honey, a land of promise for some and shattered dreams of stardom for others. For me California has been a testing ground, a proving point of sorts. A refiner's fire, California was my furnace. I've been salted by its fire, and am better for it. On this sun-drenched golden coast, I discovered and accepted the call as a groomsman of men, not knowing I'd become for many the groomsman of grooms, a best man.

Born in a modest home on the East Coast of the United States to Charles & Elsie Gooden, I was the youngest of five, a baby that was not supposed to be born. My mother had complications with my brother when she delivered him. As a result, when she became pregnant with me, it produced a dangerous scenario. The doctors had encouraged her and my father to abort me. They feared that due to medical complications, she would probably not survive the birth, and neither would I. With her life and mine compromised by this prognosis, my mother began to pray. It was later in my adult life that she revealed to me the details of my birth. My mother had a spiritual encounter that assured her the both of us would live. This gave her the strength to carry me to term. Her faith was strong and although my father insisted on aborting me, my mother held fast and trusted what G-d had told her. I was going to make it to this little blue spot in the universe called EARTH. Praise G-d of Heaven. SELAH! I made it!

Ever since my first memory, I recalled sensing an internal compass within, moving me towards the things of G-d. As early as 5 years of age I wanted my neighbors and my friends to know G-d as I did. It was a real and very personal faith for me. One encounter that stands out in my mind is one of a father of a fellow playmate. He was drunk at the time. I remember walking up to him and asking him to stop drinking, and to do it for his son. That was a bold thing to do, especially for a 5-year-old.

Both my father and mother were not particularly religious people. My father owned nightclubs. My mother was a stay-at-home mom before they separated and subsequently divorced. However, it was my mother's faith and my grandmother's intervention that became the main component and source of strength and guidance for my life.

My faith as a little boy grew, though my father rejected me and consistently attacked my beliefs. I knew G-d accepted me, and that enabled me to endure my father's abuses, physically and mentally. I learned early on in life what it meant to carry a cross. It was during this time that the faith instilled in me by my mother, and nurtured by my grandmother, empowered and grounded me. Eventually I moved past my pain, without vindictiveness or bitterness. I was learning what grace and gratitude looked like as my life was transformed by faith in Yeshua.

Grooming men started with my own house, my brothers, cousins, uncles, and friends. I would share with anyone, anywhere who would take time to listen to a little boy, one who marched to the beat of a different drummer.

From my early childhood to as recent as the late 90's I was both mentored and mentoring, always remaining open to learn and improve my commitment to others. I shared whatever I learned or experienced, never holding back.

California had become my ultimate boot camp and testing ground, as I said, my furnace. All my lessons would be tested here. They were challenged, attacked and revealed for what they truly were or were not. I revamped some ideas, entirely abandoned others, and held on to some for dear life. However, no matter how hot the fires of my testing became, I maintained my focus and purpose.

I knew that regardless of the trial or setback, the struggle or failure, I had a calling. I knew who I was and secretly guarded that deeper purpose against the dissuading opinions of others. A man with a calling should stay true to that calling, wary of venturing too far off course. Slowly and methodically I was being transformed into a man's man, a mentor, teacher, and a father figure.

Mine was a mission to restore, prepare and remind men of who they are, who they were meant to be, and what they were called to do. "The groomsman and never the groom" is a joyous adage I gladly embrace. Finding one's calling in life is itself a journey. When we walk truthfully in our purpose, our path becomes clearer; we serve our fellow man with greater effectiveness, and thereby serve ourselves as well. The contributions we make to our society, our brothers, sons and friends, is of eternal value and benefit. So as others had done for me, now I do for others.

Singleness

Some men are called to singleness, others choose it, but no matter which, as singles we ultimately serve the institution of Marriage. Singles do not glorify singleness. On the contrary, they glorify marriage. They come along side the marital tribe and support it, and serve it any way they can. They are able to give themselves to other activities and philanthropic efforts, while leaving the family the time needed for the fathers and mothers to pour into their children. Singleness can be a dispensational disposition, simply a moment, or months or years. However long it is, accepting it allows you to make the most of it.

It's not hard to lose sight of our original goal, derailing ourselves, and getting off track. I had moments and periods of distractions, and I can tell you that these can be costly, and they were for me. These distractions can backfire on those you serve and you, so avoid the detours at all costs.

9

Groom 2 – The Player

He was young, full of life and vigor and searching for direction in his life. I was drawn to his charisma and he to mine. We both connected on so many levels of our interests in language, faith and music. He needed a friend, a mentor and a father figure. His mother was a hard working woman who loved her children. I started to pour into his life all that I had learned, all that I thought could be of benefit to him.

He opened up and shared his life's stories, the pain, the anger and the feelings of abandonment. He was full of honor, and had a good sense of family, strength and Loyalty. Perhaps a bit misguided, but just a bit, he was at his core a good young man. Ricky eventually took hold of faith. Some called this a crutch, but call it what you will, for Ricky it was his lifeline, just as it has been for many young men. Ricky's life began transforming, his actions, his choices - all began to reflect this change.

He started to walk like the lion he truly was becoming, instead of the monkey he had pretended to be. I was proud of Ricky and all the progress he had made. Ricky went from timid to bold, from useless to useful and from ineffective to effective. The "Player" was now a certifiable "Man of Honor" who continues, to this day, along with his wife, grooming other men and changing the world.

It is difficult at times for an attractive man, even if he does not pursue his temptations, to stand against the temptations that pursue him. He must constantly be on his guard as to what and who is drawn to him, the motivations behind them, and ultimately their consequences.

Ricky eventually mastered those temptations, but not before they took a bite out of him. It was a hard fought battle, but he overcame. The scars of his struggles have now become the badges of his victory, and their memory serves as his reminder to never go back. Today he continues to walk in his victory with his beloved wife, Angel. He now grooms other men to become the best of their potential.

Amazing Grace

Through many dangers toils and snares,

I have already come.

'Twas Grace that brought me safe this far

And Grace will lead me home.

His grace groomed me and saved me. Now I use that same Grace to groom others. Always the Groomsman and Never the Groom, but always by His grace!

10

Groom 3 – The Lifeguard

It was a crisp, cool, fall morning in Mammoth
Mountain, California. There we were, Greg and I,
tossing our lines into Convict's Glacier Lake,
against a backdrop of blue sky and fluffy white
cotton clouds. We were fishing for trout. We were
there to refresh and reflect, as Greg had just lost
his Father to brain cancer. Dr. Bradley was a
successful brain surgeon, a good man, father
and leader in his community. The cabin in
Mammoth was a tradition that Greg had shared
many times over with his father. Now he wanted
to share that tradition with me as he grieved. I
was his moral support. He loved his father, and
his father loved him. With his father's passing,
Greg was now trying to find his way.

Determining how he would carry his father's legacy was a daunting task.

I had first met Greg on the beach, during an early morning jog on the sand on my way to The Wedge. Greg was a lifeguard at one of the towers. When I was jogging past his tower, I said a brief "Hello." It was followed by another brief word or two (exactly what they were now, I can't recall), a conversation ensued and the rest is history. Greg and I became quite close. From that day on we began to spend time as friends, hanging out, eating tacos and lemon cake (his favorite), and playing and recording music together. We even made a CD together.

We caught trout up on that mountain that day, and boy was it gooooood! Greg gutted and cleaned it (YEAH!) and I prepared it and cooked it (Yummmmmy). To this day that was truly the best trout I have ever eaten.

This was a significant turning point in the life of my friend. The passing of a father can throw a man completely off course, especially when that father is a good man. I knew the feeling all too well, as my own father had recently passed. The grief was familiar to me. However, Greg's father had honor and had lived a life full of character and integrity before his children, mine had not. I did not know what it was like to lose the likes of a man you admired and respected and strove to imitate. However, Greg did, and his pain was evident and revealing. I was privileged to know Greg and his father, as we can all become quite cynical in our worldview, believing there is no such thing as a good father. Families like the Bradley's are a beacon of hope to us who have no beacon of our own to follow. Those families tell us it's possible to be and do better, and to raise a family ourselves.

Greg valued me and reminded me of my worth to him, and made sure I knew it. Greg always had a heart for the sick and the hurting. He loved saving lives... hence being a lifeguard. Healing was in his blood, as his father had saved many lives during his medical career. Later that month I invited Greg to a banquet. I had been thinking how I could be of help to my friend, helping him sort his options and find his course. I paid for two tickets to a banquet on the Queen Mary, in Long Beach, California, where a missionary organization that does medical relief was holding an event. I felt this was his path, so I got the tickets, called him up and told him I wanted him to go to dinner with me. I hadn't told him much more than that. The organization was called Y.W.A.M. (Youth With A Mission). That night after the conclusion of the event, Greg knew what it was he must do. He asked me if I could help him pursue this, and, of course, I said yes. From that moment we began making a plan, forming a strategy, and implementing it. We raised support and off he went. Greg became a missionary to the poor and the hurting. He worked with this organization to reach indigenous groups all over the world, bringing healing in practical ways. Meeting the physical needs of children all over the world, Greg found his calling. Eventually, it took him to Australia where my friend would become the Groom and I the fulfilled groomsman.

While Greg was in Australia, I kept watch on his family here and his girlfriend as well. After a few months passed, I told Greg I thought it best he let go of the California girl and pray and keep his eyes open for another potential wife. He trusted my judgment and broke off the relationship. It wasn't long after that, when Greg ended up meeting Naomi. She too, worked with Y.W.A.M., and together they began to do the work of healing the hurting and sharing with youth all the values and lessons he had learned. Over the months, and after much counsel, Greg was persuaded that Naomi was to be his bride, and so it was and so it is. Today he is happily married with children and a wife of honor, character, beauty and charm. He is now the Groom, and now grooms others in the "Land Down Under." There is no greater joy than to see those you mentor and pour into, go on to do more than you, honoring you with their legacy of groomsman-ship. One man at a time, one groom at a time, one day at a time, there will be grooms abundant! Three down... More to go! I've got a world to cover.

11

Groom 4 - The Music Man

The music swelled, the people stood to sing, the song leader approached the podium, jubilant and smiling, raising his hands and voice.

"All creatures of our God and King, lift up your voice with me and sing, Alleluia..." Here I was at my first official job as a worship pastor! How I love music and especially the songs of my G-d. I could not help but notice the angel-faced teen in the front row. He was enveloped in the music and enjoying the singing. Most teens might be less interested, but not him. He was spiritedly participating in the worship, and I was happy to witness it - a young congregant so enthused for the music of his G-d... and no disingenuousness. Too often people of faith fall into routine and lose the spirit and meaning of what they are singing. However, this was not the case with Jonathan. I knew from that moment he was a potential groom in the making.

I spoke with him immediately after the service. He was eager to compliment me on my leadership as their new worship pastor. The pastor was a former police officer, and here I was a young African American in a relatively all white community in the Granada Hills/Simi Valley area of Southern California. Only G-d could have such a sense of humor and grace. I enjoyed my two-year pastorate there, even though I had to drive nearly 100 miles twice a week to get to the church. During that two-year mission my friendship with Jonathan grew and matured. We became inseparable as friends. He eventually joined the worship team, although he felt he had so little to offer. Of all the members on the team, he was the least experienced, and he lacked the training that the others had. However, what he lacked in training he made up in spirit and raw talent. It was an amazing addition to the team of worshippers and we were all the better for his contribution. Jonathan exceeded all our expectations. He learned from seasoned musicians and older men, who became mentors to him. His father, Pastor Jeff, was one of the associate pastors. He is one of the most honorable and principled men I know. All I could do was to add to the foundation his father and mother had already established, and what a foundation that was. Both Pastor Jeff and Nancy

Wisner were stellar examples in the area of pastoring and parenting.

As a result of my and other musicians' influence in Jonathan's life, he decided to pursue music as a career. He was mature beyond his years, and that was attributed to his being home schooled. He was himself, as his father, a man of honor and integrity, one you could trust blindly. I used my influence to reinforce the teachings of his father. His father was grateful for it and thanked me on many occasions for the role I played in his son's life.

Eventually as Jonathan got older, we became more a part of each other's lives. We hiked, cooked, and jammed together often on guitar and piano, writing songs and recording music. He was an incredible songwriter. We loved smash ball on the beach and he soon found out just how obnoxiously competitive I can be. I loved tennis, he loved basketball, which was his fathers' game. But he always preferred tennis because he knew I loved it and I preferred basketball because I knew he loved it. We always sacrificed for the good of the other. When he and his family were preparing to move away, my heart was saddened, so I asked his father if I could join him on the 30-hour drive from California to Kansas, where they had relocated. We drove a U-haul truck with their furnishings. Yahoo! It was quite the adventure and one I shall never forget. Jonathan had already arrived in Kansas. I looked at every mile as a mile closer to see my best friend, my pastor's son. When we arrived, Jonathan and I both ran into each other's arms as if we were long lost brothers. I had been writing a song along the way, just as he had before my arrival. When we met we combined our separate song ideas and once again the songwriting team of Rogers and Hammerstein, I mean, Jonathan and Steve, came up with a hit: "On The Road To Kansas." Jonathan eventually started school, pursued music and became a music major. He exceeded me in all my musical abilities. He is quite the music man now. I took many more trips to Kansas in the years following, as his father had become the pastor of a local church. Our friendship grew even deeper. Eventually he took a job in Florida, which I protested more out of personal reasons than spiritual ones. I wanted to protect my friend and I felt Kansas was a better place to potentially find a wife than Florida. However, Jonathan relocated, so now I found myself flying to Florida frequently to visit my best friend. I always supported him in his pursuits, just as I had done with his mission work in Brazil for two years. It was here in Florida that my best friend would find his wife, Lida, a vibrant, strong, friendly South-African young lady. She was an au pair for a family at the church where Jonathan played music. Now I became his best man, a groomer of the groom. I could not have been happier at the time. I was passing the baton to a greater love, a godly love that would look after the groom for life, Lida his bride. As a member of his "pride," how happy I was to stand with him that day and how happy I am to continue standing with him. He and his wife are happily married with children, their quiver ever growing. I was the groomsman but not the groom, yet ever happier in the role of seeing my best friend fulfilled and completed in marriage. Four down and still more to come - always grooming.

12

Groom 5 - The Hero, The Bear

It was one of those typical Midwestern winter
days, not too cold, when I flew into Kansas for
one of Jonathan's music events. I waited in the
auditorium as he and his team of musicians
rehearsed. Not long after I had been sitting
there, in walked a bear of a man, looking like a
combination of a GQ suit model and a man
ready to go to war. Eyes wide with observation
and with a walk like a prince, he introduced
himself as a friend of Jonathan's. He shook my
hand like the bear that he was, but smiled like
an angel bearing good news. His voice was
booming and unashamed and his presence was
fearless yet welcoming. Truly, this is what a hero
might look like. However, heroes come in all
shapes and sizes. I immediately identified with

his politics and he with mine. He was a young man eager to make an impact on his world. Little did I realize at that moment that this was groom number five. I wondered if he realized who exactly I was, always a groomsman and never the groom.

After talking for hours, we exchanged emails and eventually began visiting each other, back and forth from Kansas to California. He had been interested in a lady or two, but as the relationship between he and I deepened, I encouraged him to put his interest elsewhere. Soon after that, along came Megan. He was enamored with her. He trusted my judgments as I helped him in counsel and prayer while seeking the will of G-d for his life. We both continued to pray about his relationship with Megan. Isaac asked her a series of questions, and based on her answers, he would determine if she was to be his wife. Megan's answers were spot on, but one in particular stood out; it was when she said, "I want a man who loves God more than he loves me." Isaac, the groom-to-be, was that man, and he was happy to hear that answer. From that time on, Isaac and I began to plan his proposal event.

The proposal event we planned would take place at the famous Las Brisas restaurant in Laguna Beach, California. We chose the gazebo adjacent to the restaurant, which was perched on a bluff overlooking the mighty Pacific. It was sunset, it was warm, and it was a fairy tale engagement setting. I was the grooming groomsman and photographer; they were the bride and groom in waiting. It was glorious!

The following months I found myself back in Kansas, where my previous groom and best friend, Jonathan, had introduced me to Isaac. Jonathan and I began coordinating the music for Isaac's wedding, and Isaac would honor me by naming me his best man. Honor upon honor, reward without debt, glory, respect and strength of bond - we are brothers in arms.

These men teach me the value and purpose of singleness, permitting me to exercise my beliefs, testing my character, raising my integrity and clarifying my motives. Thank you, Isaac Boehr, Groom Five. What a Bear of a man you are. The groomsman is proud to have stood with you.

A Man's Man, A Prince

Who is my brother, who is my friend, a brother's brother, and a friend's friend? The dreams of the bride are fulfilled in the prince of her dreams. A true prince has been tried and tested by the fires of grooming. No greater love is there to be found in men such as these, than those who would lay down their lives for their friends. Grooming the groom grooms him for the bride, her husband to be, for the children that will call him father, and for the world where he will one day take his rightful place.

13

Groom 6 - The Tall One, The Director

He was as tall as a giant and as talented in film as the best of them. He had an eye for light and a good angle, and a gentle attitude to boot. We first met in the local gym. I had attempted to train him on some of the gym equipment. Eventually, we moved past working out and discovered we shared other common interests such as film and music. I was looking for an avenue to expose my music to the world (without going on American Idol). Jon and I thought about doing a music documentary of my journey as a starving artist. It wasn't long before the idea moved from conversation to storyboarding. Over the next few months Jon and I began to spend countless hours filming, editing, and planning our music documentary premier. This time spent with Jon allowed me many hours of discussion on spiritual matters. Jon had several older men in his life, not the least of which was his stepfather, Doug, whom Jon loved deeply. Still, there was something missing in Jon's life. I was able to help fill that gap, spiritually nurturing my friend. My contribution was to give him a strong spiritual compass, to direct his steps and to give him purpose. There was also a neighbor, a godly man who was a faithful father to his own children and a leader in his church and community. He, too, contributed to Jon's mentoring.

Jon met Jenny, the quintessential California girl, kissed by "the golden sun" and bathed in the salt of California's oceanic waves. She was the fragrance of Jasmine and the song of the morning sparrows. She was all Jon desired and all he wanted. They eventually moved in together. They were happy, but they were not married. Too often in our society we are more elated with the image of a home rather than the actual building of one. Many prefer the facade, the Hollywood set, a prop with no substantive material behind it. A home is a couple's covenant dwelling, a sanctuary from a confused and chaotic world. This is a society that tells us good is evil, and evil is good, a society that glories in the violations of our daughters and sisters, making them only fodder for the sexual appetite of young men, or a trophy for older men. A home built on a poorly laid foundation can never stand the pressures of time or the winds of an antithetical culture, which is all the more why we need to establish sound spiritual and moral principles at the beginning of a relationship.

In this present generation, men have a near empty pond in which to fish. Not only is it poorly stocked, it is poorly kept, and not very diverse. Once, I was sitting in a church service when the pastor asked for anyone who wanted a husband to come down for prayer. Four women stood up in front of me to go down. One of them looked back towards me and said, "I'm going to get me a husband." I stopped the sisters before they left the pew, and said gently, "Sisters, it's best to ask the Lord to prepare you to be a wife first before you pray for a husband." Equally, men should do the same – they should prepare the inner nest of their pride, before they hunt for a bride. The most important quality that women should look for in their potential husbands is the development of the inner man. If the inner nest is well prepared, the outer nest is no problem.

I asked Jon who had given him Jenny. He said he felt she was a gift from God. I then asked him, "How would you treat a gift from a king or a queen of a nation? Would you treat it as if you had found it in a trash can in an alley, or as if a derelict had given you it? Of course not! Instead, you would display it in the most cherished place of honor in your home. You would protect it. You would clean it. You would be proud to tell others about it. So, you should treat Jenny in the same way, for she is worth more than a gold statue or a fancy coat, fast cars, motorcycles or the latest gadget." A woman and children are the highest gifts to a man. They are not to be abused, misused, or dishonored. A properly groomed man knows and understands that his right actions will produce good results. I said, "Treat Jennifer like a gift from heaven, not a curse from hell. Value her, honor her, and do not partake of her love without a ring, a covenant, a promise, and a vow. Treat her as you would want your daughter, sister, or very own mother treated. A famous pop singer once said, 'Single ladies put a ring on it'. Make her an honorable woman, by honorably marrying her."

We have allowed too many of our daughters to appear as unpaid streetwalkers. They are not, and should never be treated that way. They should be treated as women of honor. Women of honor are ingenious, industrious and pleasant, guarded and yet hospitable, moral, respectful, strong yet humble. Each is a queen in her own right, in her own home, amongst her own family.

I am happy to say that Jon proposed to Jenny, and the two of them wasted no time resetting their moral compass and their moral destination - they got married. Months later, we had the ceremony in the back yard of her mother's house. The mother of the groom thanked me for having the courage to speak to her son boldly, encouraging him to step up and do the right thing.

At times it may be difficult to be the fly in the ointment of worldly wisdom, but if you can endure the persecution, the outcome may yield a great reward. We must be willing to speak up and out about those values and principles that are true, without regard to what others may think. If not you, then who? If not here, then where? If not now, then when? It must be you – be a standard bearer.

On I go to another man. Time for the groomsman to groom another groom.

14

Grooming Principles

The following is what I call the syllabus of wrong grooming; let's take a look at its curriculum.

Wrong Grooming Principles

1. *Be Tough* = Manly

2. *Don't Cry* = Emotion is a feminine trait

3. *Fight* = Force before diplomacy and reason

4. *Take It* = Be quiet, say nothing, keep mouth shut

5. *Be Athletic* = Youth at any cost, focus on sports and body

6. *Talk Rough* = Use threatening, harsh, and hard words

7. *Be Stylish* = Dress like an image - reflect the cultural crowd

8. *Be a Player* = Live like a ladies' man, impress your fellow player

9. *Pursue Sex* = Live by the lust of the flesh

10. *Play and Party* = Be reckless, throw caution to the wind, ignore consequences

11. *Make Lots of Money* = Cheat, steal, deceive, connive - anything to make more

12. *Grab Power* = Be served rather than serve

These 12 principles have been followed religiously for generations, a time cherished practice that many fathers have passed down to their sons. Yet look around you. What do you see? What has this gotten us? It hasn't worked. Rather, it has left men still boys at 40, and others at 17 looking to belong, so they join gangs. When abandoned by their fathers, our sons abuse girls, and our daughters abuse themselves or are abused by others, sleeping with many boys while in and out of relationships and marriages. Let's answer these with the right grooming principles.

Right Grooming Principles

1. *Be Strong* = Face fears reasonably and with courage

2. *Express Yourself* = Release emotions healthily - don't bottle them or hold them in

3. *Be Patient* = Observe, then discern the right action and act

4. *Endure* = Bear up under pressure and don't run from every difficulty

5. *Be Healthy* = Eat well, exercise moderately, adopt a healthy lifestyle

6. *Communicate* = Words are power - use good vocabulary

7. *Be Modest* = Dress age-appropriately and presentably

8. *Be Honorable* = Keep your word, make few vows, and follow through

9. *Be Moral* = Resist temptation, make a weak moment a strong one

10. *Be Joyful* = laugh, smile, play. Life can be hard - take time to have fun responsibly

11. *Be Productive* = Work with your hands, do it well, don't be lazy

12. *Lead* = Be humble, serve more than you are served, give more than you take

Grooming the groom does not always result in a marriage ceremony. In fact, in most instances it results in an ending of relationships and the refocusing of one's own need to be redeemed.

Most of us are not ready or prepared for a relationship, much less a wedding. We spend too much of our lives looking to others either to fulfill us or to blame them for what they did or did not do. Our lives are like scattered electrons, in disarray following no particular order, no sequence, and no rule of law. Truly grooming the groom requires a total reworking and revamping of one's life philosophies. We cannot give away what we ourselves do not possess, we cannot teach what we have not learned, and we cannot lead where we have not followed. We must learn how to groom ourselves and then to allow others to groom us.

Identify and know who you are, who God created you to be. Know your family heritage and history - it reveals much. Decide what translates into definable words, words that identify your vocation and your person. Learn to own who you are. Embrace it - it's an inalienable truth and fact whether you like it or not. Seek out like-minded people who share your worldview, and are not afraid to challenge your thinking. You will attract what you are, so work at that which you want to be, and convey it. When making vows, don't be hasty, but keep the ones you make. Be trustworthy, work your routine and follow through. In your patience, whether young or old, understand the joy of delayed gratification but celebrate the reward of a good action, for we reap what we sow. In the end, leave your legacy, something of yourself that others can model and build upon. Enrich them with your experiences, so that they don't have to reinvent the wheel.

If a man attends to himself he will allow others to attend to him also. It will result in an extra pair of eyes. It will reinforce and strengthen you, especially in weak moments. Men, welcome this, it holds us accountable, not to others, but to ourselves. Stay on the path – it's your moral grid. It keeps you within the margins of your life's course, never straying too far. Fly like an airplane - only off course marginally, but generally steady on course.

The people you choose or attract will either make you better or bitter. In healthy grooming, the tools that you use matter. Be careful of those who will groom you according to their own image and identity. Choose instead, groomers that reflect the highest and best standards and ideals, exceeding the minimum measures of others.

> ## To Thine Own Self Be "Groom"
>
> Identify who you are.
>
> Define what that means and what it is.
>
> Rework the worst of it.
>
> Apply it and become it.
>
> Welcome those who constructively critique.
>
> Be compatible.
>
> Be consistent, with good behaviors and routines.
>
> Be patient, act with wisdom and discernment.
>
> Leave a legacy - pass it on.

The Anatomy of Grooming - Taming The Four Beasts

Recognize your own inner structure, how you are quartered in your challenges. The following are the four areas of the anatomy of grooming:

The Brain

The Belly

The Heart

The Loins

"The Brain" refers to your academic mind – intellect and reasoning. "The Belly" refers to your wanting, your hungering, and your appetites for physical matter. "The Heart" refers to your feelings, your passions, and your desires. "The Loins" refers to your lusts, your sexuality, your youth, and your folly.

These four "beasts" - each in themselves are a formidable challenge to the groom. Before one can truly become a groom, well groomed, he must face one, if not all, of the four "beasts." Men may not be weak in all of these four areas, but will typically succumb to one or a combination of them. It is our "Achilles heel."

The "brain beast" is probably equal in power to the "loin beast." Men are often driven by their sexual prowess, hence the anthropological conclusions that man procreates at any and all expense. Equally, at any and all expense, man seeks to understand and is never satisfied with not knowing. Hence, the constant search, quest for discovery, and need to hypothesize.

Though the "belly beast" and the "heart beast" are not as powerful as the other two, they should, nonetheless be taken seriously. The "belly beast" is infamous for throwing a man off-track or blinding him completely to the clear vision of his destiny. This is accomplished by the sheer hungering for power, position and possessions. Ancient kings and warriors alike have been their own demise by following their insatiable thirst to either take more than they should take, want more than they should want, or have more than they can carry. The "belly beast" causes the obesity of our body through food and drink, leading to sickness, disease and drunkenness, or an inability to secure (maintain, manage, control) what we possess because the sheer abundance of our possessions possesses us.

Lastly, the "heart beast" ironically plays ping-pong or racquetball. He bounces off the "brain beast," the "belly beast," and the "loin beast," using all three to accomplish his goal. This beast wants you to follow whatever suits him best. If the intellect is in play, the loins will say that you don't need to follow what you cannot reason, understand or comprehend. The problem with that reasoning is that not every right action can be rightly understood or comprehended. The "heart beast" is counting on that. When the "heart beast" is unsuccessful in using your intellect to derail the groom-in-the-making, he will bounce off the "belly beast," hoping that your appetite for what fills your eyes with want will throw you off course. In Greek mythology we see many tales of men lured by enchanting sirens, and that can be in search of a treasure – a woman, a meal or something far more esoteric. Many Hollywood movies have played this scenario over and over again in their plots with politicians, police officers, and government spies alike being bought off by either money, blackmail, sex, power, or possessions.

Finally, the "loin beast" is the most precise arrow in his quiver of three. This has, in fact, destroyed more grooms-in-the-making and grooms than either of the other two. This particular "beast" says, "If it feels good, do it!" It is all about the passion and elation of physical ecstasy. Historically as well, many great kings, soldiers, celebrities and ordinary men have fallen to, or were led away by, their lusts. The groom-to-be, as well as the groom, must be fully armed, and once armed to tame these four beasts, must never take off his armor, for these beasts are never killed, but can only be tamed. It is a constant working of the will, despite the good fight of faith against these four, until the day you die, until through death you depart.

Society has answered this already. It's screamed from every orifice of media. We are surrounded and repeatedly bombarded with what our view should be by these prophets of culture. Much of the understanding we as men walk away with is best described in words as "muscularized masculinity." This term emphasizes our lack of true masculinity via a cacophony of misguided attempts to obtain true manhood. When void of true strength we resort to our beggarly instincts like Neanderthals, mindlessly roaming about, telling ourselves that animal-like machismo is what defines a man. Yes, some of this "muscularizing" is, or can be, normal. By some accounts, it's a product of testosterone. However, like everything else in our bloated culture today, it is indicative of the extreme, obsessive and overindulgent approach that is typically our modus operandi.

A Groom-less Soliloquy

We groom with piercings and tattoos,
Harleys and cars,
Jewelry, jeans, cash and gold bars.
Then it's the women with our winnings
We start to attract,
While dressed in our suits,
We think there's nothing we lack.
Yet while locked in our cells,
We hopelessly pursue,
The youth that once was,
The fool that was you.
Blinded by "better" (so we think that we are),
Truthfully speaking we've not gone very far.
We've become bitter and battered
At the end of the day.
Is there not one stalwart man left standing,
Have we all gone astray?

Let's not make that soliloquy true; let's start
by renaming both you and me.

15

Groom 7 – The Roommate

I have always been drawn to water. I recall that as a child, while at the beach in Atlantic City, New Jersey, I went too far out into the ocean for my size and nearly drowned. Thankfully my father saw me and rescued me. My mother reminds me of it to this day. From that moment, I've had a love-hate relationship with water. I swim, but not often enough to be good at it. But how I love the ocean and how it calls to me. It's no wonder that I've always found surfers as friends, and have attempted on several occasions to surf myself, but to no avail. In self-grooming we often attract those who can aid in the elimination of both our fears and inhibitions, consciously or subconsciously.

I've always wanted to live near the ocean, so I sought out a roommate near the Newport Beach pier. "The right roommate" - now that would be the real challenge. One time, I thought I had found him. His name was Roger. At our first meeting he seemed honest, trustworthy and dependable, having a wonderful disarming way about him, like the Wisconsonian that he was. I admired that quality in him. He assured me he lived alone and did not have a girlfriend living with him.

Soon after moving in, the man who would later become quite a good friend of mine was still a stranger. I discovered he had not fully disclosed that he had a girlfriend.

Apartment life in California is expensive, so you do what you need to do in order to live here. But how could I teach others these lessons, living in a situation that appeared to condone the opposite? "What we say matters, but what we do even more so." These are simple truths in the grooming of ourselves and others. It is a constant lifelong commitment, grooming and being groomed.

Like a groom choosing a bride, we look for a job, a company to employ us. We date it, investigate it and then decide to make a commitment to it, which may last the rest of our life, but more likely only a few years. In this modern world, rarely does anyone commit to a firm for life. Companies are no more vested or interested in a long-term relationship with you than you are interested in a long-term relationship with them. This is, in fact, a perfect mirror of relationships between men and women today. We skip around, because there is no commitment. We all want the affair! We can jump ship and "marry" another company, in the event of a better job offer.

With Roger and his girlfriend, there was no contract, no long-term commitment and no investment. I was seeing it play out right in front of me. It was here that I encouraged Roger to do the honorable thing. "Marry her!" Roger really loved Erika, so after much pressure and peer influence, motivated by my sincere love for both he and Erika, they got married.

To this day, Roger, Erika and their two boys Cody and Kaiden continue living as a model family. They are loving parents and pillars in their community. That great institution of "marriage and family" now has new members, and I have become "Uncle Steve."

Not Always a Groomsman,
Not Always the Groom

There are failures, mishaps, mistakes and errors along the way, and I have made many myself. It is a cost to pay for these lessons, often learned on the backs of others. I penned this book to minimize the mishaps and mistakes, so that others might do better than I. This is my legacy, stand on my shoulders if you dare, and go build a greater one.

For every successful grooming of a groom, there is the groomsman that never made it or that never showed up. Our lessons are hard to learn. This is in part due to a lack of will to learn them and apply them, or to a lack of the discipline to maintain them. The strongest or the fastest does not always win the races we run in this life, but often those who persevere to the end win them. Mankind has always found that where there is a will there is a way. If we don't see a way, we make one, find one or become one, whether going around the mountain, over the mountain, under the mountain, or tunneling through the mountain. As archaic as much of this will sound to some readers, it is a timeless truth that many of our fathers have failed to teach and instill in us. For every lost generation, there will arise someone unique to the task of grooming - a Gideon, a Ruth, a David, a Churchill, a Reagan - someone least amongst us, unexpected, who will re-awaken his generation. What once was considered old now will be made new again, re-kindling the fires that groom great men.

16
Groom 8 – On The Mountain Top

To many, marriage is a mountaintop experience, an arrival to the pinnacle of blissful success.

I took a new job. It was a boiler room atmosphere, but a job nonetheless. I had found out through a friend named Caleb that there was an opening in his company. I first met Caleb through a common friend. What I recall is the stylishly tailored man that Caleb was. He and his girlfriend Tiffany both looked like they had just walked off the pages of a magazine cover. They appeared to be the perfect couple, aesthetically speaking. But honestly, Caleb and

Tiffany were also two of the nicest people I knew, two of the sweetest people I had come to know. Nonetheless, thanks to the Sunny California lifestyle, this beautifully humble couple was unmarried and living together like so many others. I grew attached to both Caleb & Tiffany, and began to share with them the richness of the truth of a groom and a bride and their proper conduct. I spent considerable time with them, and as time went on, I emphasized the value of honor and integrity. "Put a ring on her finger," I said. "It will be a symbol of your honor and commitment." This symbol of your love screams to a glaring world, "This is a woman of worth, one that is spoken for." He agreed, and I went from being a groomsman to being asked to marry them. It would be the first wedding that I would be officiating, and it would be atop a mountain. However, this was not just any mountain. The road to the top was the most dangerously precipitous road I had ever driven. The wedding chapel was deep in California's Death Valley. There we went, my co-driver Leo and I, up the winding rail-less road. We were thousands of feet above the desert floor, inching along, while fearing a plunge to death. My palms were sweating, dripping with uneasiness. In comparison, the gang-ridden streets of downtown Los Angeles seemed so much safer than my present situation.

That was the year that I was the sickest I'd ever been. I felt like I was at death's door, a result of a flu epidemic that had gripped southern California with a vengeance. It was a violent infection that lasted for nearly 75 days and kept me bed-ridden much of the time. I had to be waited on hand and foot, but nothing helped except the kindness of Kathy and Carl who were looking after me, and the time needed for the virus to run its course. Nearly 3 months of no work, and a year to recover my voice. As I was beginning to recover my strength, Caleb and Tiffany's wedding day was fast approaching. I had to make the trip through Death Valley. As I mentioned earlier, my Argentinean friend Leo agreed to help me make the drive. Even with that, I barely made it. Caleb and Tiffany anxiously awaited my arrival, determined to have me conduct their ceremony. It was one of the highest honors I had ever received... thank you!

It was a beautiful mountaintop wedding in that blistering summer heat, and the chapel was sweltering. I set a new benchmark for sweaty noses, but by the Grace of God, I was able to endure it. After the wedding, I thought to myself, "The groom has been groomed... I'm out of here!" But then we had to go back down that precipitous mountain road, which brings me to another point. Mountain Climbers. How do they climb 15,000' peaks and higher? Is it for glory that they endure such challenges to the human body? Or is it the bragging rights, to boast that they went, they saw, they conquered? Even after the euphoria of climbing a mountain, one still has to face the ire of the return down that difficult path. Many Tibetans have made the trek across the Himalayas on spiritual pilgrimages. For the few that have made it to the top, even fewer survive the trek back. For me the real fear isn't the trek to the top, it's the descent. Once I reached my goal, I had to immediately begin planning my return. Many marriages are similar in this way. They start at the base of the mountain of their relationship's towering peaks, excited about the trek to the top. Once there, however, the elation is short-lived and begins to fade away. There is no room on the mountaintop to pitch a tent for habitation. Consequently, there is disappointment, and then the joy of the journey to that blissful peak is forgotten. Immediately they begin to head back down the mountain of what once had been a joy to climb. They start to settle in for their descent. Down they go into the dismal abyss of failure and divorce, a divided house with divided children. Usually they end up even lower than the point from which they began. Many don't even make it halfway down, before the entire relationship dies along the way. Others now pass their remains as a monument or memorial of failed dreams, filling them with fear and cynicism, as they ask themselves, "What happened?" This doesn't have to be a tragic ending; instead we can make it a triumphant resurrection of what we feared was lost forever. Just like the mountain climbers who attempt to cross the Himalayas, one can learn from both those who climbed and returned and those who climbed and fell. We can repeat their successes and avoid their pitfalls and failures.

Remember, when traversing mountains, it's the Donkey in a man that's best at navigating those treacherous turns, bends, narrow spaces and rocks. Don't plan on descending, when climbing your marital mountain. Take a scorched-earth policy. Make no "plan B" or concessions for failure. Burn the bridge of return, pitch a tent, and own your mountain! Eliminate the option to return to singleness. Be devoted, devout, till death do you part. Determine in your mind "Divorce is not an option." Eliminate that word from your vocabulary. Even Jesus said that the Law of Moses, which had provisions for divorce, was not written because God desired it, but rather, written because of the hardness of men's hearts. (Matthew 19:8)

17
Groom 9 – Oregon

Off to another mountain, only this time, it's the mountain ranges of Shasta, California. I drove nearly 30 hours from Southern California to Oregon to visit Joel at his college in Portland. When I was music leader at his church in Southern California, Joel was 9 or 10 years old. Now in college and all grown up, he and I had developed quite a friendship over the years. He saw me as one of his mentors. He wanted to spend time with me, and introduce me to someone he had met, who he thought could be the one for him to marry.

Joel and I had shared many experiences over the years. After driving nearly 1,000 miles from southern California to Portland, my tires were bald and my tush was numb. I did not sit for a week. We spent several days together, exploring his campus and even more so, exploring the pristine, Jurassic-esque area along the Columbia River and Multnomah Falls. The Northwest region of the U.S. seems to take you back in time. It is easy to see why some people are tempted to worship the creation, rather than the Creator.

Eventually I was introduced to Christina, the object of his affection. She was a beautiful young lady, strong in spirit. I advised him not to rush, but pray and pray continually regarding proposing to her. It wasn't long before Joel settled on the fact that Christina was indeed the one he wanted to spend the rest of his life with. Soon after the proposal, the wedding day was upon us. It seemed overnight, and the groom I had been grooming was about to take his bride. Success! Although I did not physically stand with Joel on his wedding day, I had been standing with him his whole life.

18

Groom 10 – The Thinker

I have reserved one last story for this book - my friend, my brother, my confidant, and my good man, Tarp. I had first met him on a pizza delivery, a delivery made from my favorite pizza place on the Newport peninsula, Laventina's Pizza (The Big Cheese). There he came up the stairs, a knock on the door, then that face. Wild yet studied, fresh yet troubled, a dutiful expression without prejudice, all this I could see as he stood there with my favorite pizza (extra sauce, green peppers, pineapple and pepperoni with light cheese). He saw my guitar leaning against the wall, and asked if I played. I answered that I did, but not well. He said he played also. We talked and discovered we were both from the East Coast, and were both excited about that. After his shift ended, that very night, he returned to visit me and we played music, spoke of our deeply rooted faith, and made arrangements to meet again. Our friendship grew and we both began studying the Bible together, playing tennis, breaking bread in fellowship, and of course, playing music. Tarp and I became the closest of friends. He was attending one of our local private Christian universities. His major was language (Spanish) and he wanted to be a teacher. At this time he had a girlfriend who attended the same university as he. Tarp wanted to grow deeper in his understanding in a way he had not before. He wanted to be certain that marrying Alysia was God's desire for him, and not just his own desire. We spent many walks together, discussing the various questions, seeking answers that our faith provided. I have come to realize that the time-old practice of men walking, talking, and just being together has been forsaken by this present generation. No meaningless conversation crept up as we spoke about the issues of our day. We avoided the typical speech of men engaged in loud exchanges over recent sporting events. In grooming ourselves and others, it is productive to have meaningful, intimate reflection while meditating and discussing things beneficial to our hearing. Notwithstanding, levity and trivial conversation does serve a purpose at times as well. Tarp had many questions and was at a stage where he was respectfully analyzing and questioning everything, even his own beliefs. It was during this time that I was able to get to know him better - his uniqueness and his passion.

With wisdom I prayed for discernment in how to counsel him. I cannot claim I was perfect in this. However, I was diligent in giving him what was my best at the time, with the purest of intentions. Alysia, his girlfriend, was growing restless and not without cause, for she and Tarp had been dating for a considerable length of time. She was close to completely throwing away the hope of ever becoming his wife. I encouraged him to come to a decision, feeling compassion for the woman waiting painstakingly in the shadows for his proposal.

The moment seemed it would never arrive. One evening on what I have come to call our "Man date" (brother's night out) we ate at an Indian/Asian style café on the campus of UCI. It was there at that dinner, as we discussed our plans for the weekend, that the groom made himself known. I recall asking him if he was free to catch a movie that I wanted to see. He said sure. It was customary for us to see movies, as I am a bit of a movie buff. He then asked if Alysia could join us, and I said sure. I did enjoy being around the both of them as I observed the manner in which they conducted themselves publicly. They were classy at all times. He, however, did repeat the confirmation that she could come along, but this time he used a different word in describing her. "I'm glad my fiancé can come along," he said cavalierly. I replied, "What?" in astonishment. At first hearing, that almost went past me. After all, I had no reason to suspect he had proposed to her. I lifted my head and said again, "What?" He replied "You know, my fiancé, Alysia." The tears began to swell in my eyes. For a moment I lost sight of my friend sitting before me. I could not believe what I was hearing. The food arrived and the waitress must have been confused, two men sitting together and one of them clearly overtaken with emotion. The elation for Alysia was what made me rejoice, weep and celebrate. My friend and brother whom I had been grooming had stepped up. Yippee! I can be a groomsman again! I was happy for Alysia, and proud of him for having done what needed to be done. I was happy that a woman so in love with him with divine purity and intention was ready to become his wife, and that he was ready to become her groom. Prayer answered. Now on to the wedding! Tarp and Alysia's union was a stellar testimony of love, patience, and faith - a credit to both, and a testimony of those that had been grooming them all their lives. What a glorious outcome, always grooming the groom and never the groom. What a calling! So inexpressible is my joy and gratitude, no matter how great or small the role I play. No wonder I can say with sincerity and contentment... "Always a Groomsman and Never the Groom" and proud of it! I love my job!

19

The Bachelor Party

Our culture prides itself on the foolish worldly wisdom of throwing caution to the wind when having bridal and bachelor parties. Bachelor parties have become infamous for being one final act of reckless behavior without moral boundaries. It's considered a last hurrah to the hedonistic, single lifestyle. A better preparation for the groom is an honorable night of reflection as he prepares to transition from singleness to marital status. Diving headfirst into a night of revelry while reliving the irresponsible acts of youthful folly does not make ready for a groom-to-be.

One of the groomsmen who flew out for Tarp's wedding, oddly enough, would soon find himself in a grooming moment. He was 6'6", a giant of a man, with compassionate eyes and a strong voice. As we moved from the suite where the party was being held and into the Jacuzzi where we all continued to talk, it was there that Trey began to share with me about himself. He explained that he flew here with his girlfriend to attend the wedding. I asked him why he had come to an honorable wedding and was going to desecrate it with a dishonorable action. He was curious what action I was referring to. I said it was being here with his girlfriend. "She's not your wife and a man should not travel to or with a woman, unless there is a covenant, or at least an engagement." I asked if he wanted to marry her. He said he intended to. "What's the delay?" I replied. He said, "Waiting to get a ring." "Is that all?!" I asked. He said, "Yes." "O.K., then let's go get her a ring." "I can't afford it!" he responded. This is what I call the classic "man-delay" and I'm not talking about a hotel in Vegas.

Top Six Man-delays

- Waiting to buy a ring.
- Wanting to buy a house first.
- Getting my finances in order.
- Not wanting to end up divorced.
- Wanting to be certain
- Waiting to finish school and get a degree.

Much of this sounds somewhat reasonable; however, when looking deeper you discover the real reasons.

- Scared
- Lack of commitment
- Scared
- Lack of Commitment
- Scared
- Lack of Commitment

... Shall I go on? I think you get the point! In life, when one is not willing to risk the loss of defeat or failure, he is equally unwilling to risk the rewards of success and victory.

I went on to tell Trey I knew one of the top jewelry brokers in the area, and that whichever ring he liked, I could get ½ off or the best price possible. My contact was a man named Brad Mugar, a good man, a family man, honorable, trustworthy, and full of integrity. I called him immediately. I told him the situation and asked if he could help me find a ring for Trey (whom I had just met). He said no problem, so I made arrangements that night to drive Trey to his business the following day and purchase a ring. Trey stepped up! He got the ring and during Tarp's wedding for which he was a groomsman, he proposed to his new bride to be. They have since been married and, ironically, Tarp flew back east for his wedding, just as Trey had done for him.

The effect we have on our peers can be good or bad. I hope this story of a random meeting with a fellow groomsman I had never met inspires you to speak words worthy of others' hearing. We should never remain silent when able to offer sound advice and good counsel. Never sit idly by and allow those with less integrity and honor to take your sons and brothers, friends and acquaintances, and lead them down the road ill advisedly. Be willing to be ready and vigilant in influencing others for righteousness sake. Though oftentimes your advice and counsel may not be easily and readily received at the moment, given time and space, one's words are often proved meritorious to the one who received them, if they are willing.

A man once said, "All it takes for evil to prosper is for good men to do nothing." Groomsmen - do something! Groom for righteousness and change your world one groom at a time.

To some degree, whether single or married, we are all called to do what we can in grooming our fellow man. Pour into them principles of truth. Cause your sons to rise up and become husbands, fathers and leaders. This is my request as the one who is always a groomsman and never the groom – groom for the prize of the bride. We press towards the mark of the High Calling! To groom or not to groom – that is the question.

20

A Groomsman's Dream

There are no perfect people, no perfect politicians, preachers, churches, heroes, athletes, soldiers, fathers, mothers, husbands and wives, sons and daughters, not even a perfect pet. No perfect day or perfect meal, perfect sunset or sunrise - no real ideal moment or perfect situation. Although we speak this way about all of the above so loosely in our everyday conversations, there is something or someone who is perfect! He that is perfect is He who created us all. He is G-d and it is my hope that every groom realizes that He who is perfect will perfect in each of us all that is lacking, to perform His good will and good pleasure, for our good and His purpose.

Strive and work towards giving your best! It is enough to resolve in ourselves that our best is to be given without complaint or compromise, so do it! "Always a Groomsman and Never the Groom" is a celebration of the legacy of passing down the principles of grooming that allow us to achieve our highest and best according to our pre-designed and pre-determined purpose ordained by our Creator. Giving ourselves to this end is an oblation to G-d.

Take time to look inwardly, to discover where grooming is needed. Dream a world where your father was present and be present in your world, a world where he was faithful and likewise be faithful in yours. Dream a world where he provided for you and you provide for your own; where he was respected and you live with respect. Dream a world in which he led with honor and truth, and you go and lead with honor and truth; a world where he loved, and now, you love! Dream a legacy and build one. Dream a fortune and give it away. Dream a future and leave it to your sons and daughters that they may continue to groom as grooms of your grooming.

A significant portion of my life has been spent pouring into the lives of others, desiring to see them fulfilled, in only what G-d ordained objectives do order the course of things. However, the one thing I've desired most has eluded me by either my own choice or my "calling"; singleness has robbed me of a son. Just one son, to pour into all that I am, all I've learned and experienced that is worthy of leaving a legacy to. To have a son and groom that boy, is the greatest calling in a man's' life. To hear the word "Father," of that man it is said that he is one who has everything. Grooming a son to carry your legacy, your dreams and push them further, drive them deeper and make them wider than you ever did, is a father's dream.

It's a Fete de Complete, when a man is properly groomed. He rises to the occasion, challenging any opponent, seeking justice and mercy, and fervently pursuing righteousness. This man gives liberally of all he possesses, even of himself if need be, while serving his fellowman with loyalty and compassion.

Throughout the years of my grooming grooms, the joy and elation of the countless weddings (not all mentioned in this book), and the tears, have been plenty. At times the heartache has been tremendous, and the battles tumultuous. I have burned bridges I shouldn't have and left others I should've burned. The inward battles of motives and ambition, regret and confusion, have more than blurred a few lines and left me dangling in no man's land, in utter dismay. The scars of these years are the only way one knows a ship has been at war. These scars, however, tell the story of where I've been, what I've done, and how I've overcome. Now the hair is grayer but the mind wiser, the heart beats slower but is battle tested, and I'm now a certified "survivor" of youth! I now have something worthy to pass on. Those who contributed to my life have played their roles, just as I have. I call these people "friends for thought" or, in the case of this book, "grooms for thought."

21

Grooms for Thought

Friends For Thought

By Steven Fitzgerald Gooden-Champ

Inspiration comes of people past and present. How would I or could I have, save 'twas not for those who are as myself fleeting thoughts upon the eternal circle of life, that rise for the morning and are laid to rest for eternity's morrow.

Indeed, these temporal beings, known as mankind play an essential role to the credit of my works. I duly welcome whatever inviting or intrusive fellows, not preferring the latter however, that I in all am to be complete in task and duty, plan and purpose, for what G-d ordained objectives do order the course of

things. May these who are to me unknown,
along this question-filled and puzzling journey,
be all the more as the invited ones I've met and
yet; let wisdom dictate that which I distaste for
higher reasons I submit.

Let this be my resolve - a chant of gratitude, for
many an inspiring fellow, none more admired
have I as you. A picture of Him, who indeed
masterminds my acquaintances and assigns me
my purposeful existence, duty and destiny.

From time to time a young man emerges to
show us the way, but that is the exception. Let's
not forget that it is the aged, old wines of
humanity that lead us in right paths with
integrity. Being older should result in a wiser
state, but this is not always the case. Let's make
it true that what was once said of old men, might
be said again, *"Wisdom resides with the aged."*
The first century Roman philosopher Seneca
said *"Nothing is more dishonorable than an old
man, heavy with years, who has no other
evidence of his having lived long except his age."*

Grooming the groom is a simple act of
teaching and mentoring, learning to live the
mundane well before you take on the complex!
Seneca said, *"For even to live is an act of
courage."*

Never acquiesce. Seneca said, *"The bravest
sight in the world is to see a great man struggling
against adversity."* I however would say,

"The bravest sight in our modern world, is to see a man struggle against mediocrity."

It was Albert Einstein who said, *"Try not to become a man of success, but rather try to become a man of value."* Be about the business of men, and men will then be about their business. Micah 6:8 says it best, *"...to act justly, love mercy and walk humbly with God."*

There is no obstacle capable of preventing us from achieving the higher good, than that of a man's own will. Therefore, says Aeschylus, the Greek Dramatist, *"When a man's willing and eager, even the god's join in to help him."* Jesus, the Son of G-d (Moshiach), said if any would follow him, he then must take up his cross and deny himself. Most of us want glory without a fight, riches without labor, and joy without tears. I would say, it's not the burden of the cross that causes people to buckle under its weight, but rather the will to bear it! Where there is a will there will be made a way.

22
A Groomsman's Commission

Not all will accept the call to groom. This is reserved for the committed and the willing, the morally minded and the strong in heart (1 Peter 5:1-14). If you choose to answer this call, or desire to, then understand it comes with responsibilities that require perseverance. It is noble and purposeful to elect to carry such a burden. Rest assured however, it's no cakewalk. For every one man groomed, there were 99 more that were not willing to answer the call. However, for the ones who did, grooming them was a joy, so do it with joy! The call to turn the hearts of the children to their fathers and the father's hearts to their children and their duty, while reconciling and redeeming what was lost, will rebuild our societal pillars. Run with your sons, giving them wings to fly higher than you ever did, and feet to run faster than you ever did, teaching them not to become weary in well-doing, but to be both diligent and vigilant. Like the African Pelican, to your sons, give of your life that they may live to thrive and flourish, fulfilling their purpose and destiny.

Daily Routine

Remind: Remind yourself who you are. Remind yourself of your purpose. Remember who mentored and fathered you and the name you bear. Names are powerful. Know your name.

Re-evaluate: Examine your motives and intentions. Constantly adjust your goal, timetables, and processes.

Review: Go over the lessons already learned, stay with the basics, and remember the foundational and fundamental principles, rules, and precepts that keep you grounded.

Rebound: Bounce back from difficult moments. Rebounding ensures that you never give in, never give up, and never turn back.

Re-do: Repent of mistakes and errors. Don't let pride prevent you from stepping back and making things right. Ask and give forgiveness.

Rejoice: Duty for duty's sake can only take you so far. Desire puts the heart in the duty and if your heart is in it, you will be too.

Relax: Change what you can when you can. Learn to let go when needed.

Receive: Accept teaching from others. Allow those you mentor and father to lead.

Relish: Reflect on your success, enjoy the fruit of your work with gratitude.

Reward: Compliment, congratulate, praise and reward your men for a job well done. Commemorate their accomplishments.

Remain: Be steady, immovable, always abounding in what you know is true and right. Do not falter or waiver. Stay the course.

Reconnaissance: Keep your eyes open to potential grooms in waiting. Some will be obvious to you, others will not.

Motto

One groom at a time, then the prize of the bride, and the pride of the prize. Grooming the grooms to change the world.

Groomsman Gratitude

I've not had a father to teach me, being a product of a divorced family. But I did have fathers, men who poured into my life, men who dared to challenge me in my arrogance, my ignorance, and my ambivalence. Men who were patient with me, believed in me, and invested in me their time, life, love, and resources. I hope my life is a reflection of all their lessons and teachings. They taught me and I pray I can do as they did.

Thank you, Gracias, Mahalo, Merci, Graci:

Pastor Robert Walls, Shaji Matthews, Rev. Pervis Story, Pastor Clifford Young, Bill, Dan Scalf, Arch Cook, Freeman Chambers, Dr. D. James Kennedy, Carl Nagy, Ray Turner, Brad Mugar, Barry Saywitz, Michael Saywitz, Dr. Doug Tarpley, Duran Potter, Lee Johnson, Stan Yoder, Pastor Jeff Wisner, Pastor Ron Seidel, Richard Dagress, Tammy and Patrick Welter, Jonathan Tarpley, Joshua Wisner, Karl Lofgren and last but not least, my Soner.

I am thankful for all you men, imperfect as you may be. Each of you still perfectly takes time with me. You taught me, fed me, helped me, led me, and freed me to achieve my best potential. You trusted me with the commission to go and to do what you did, raising men to raise children, who will rise up and call them blessed, just as I have risen to call each of you!

To my biological father who has passed away: Thank you for giving me life! Your example to me has mainly shown me what not to do, who not to be and to do and live a better life, hopefully restoring and regaining the honor of a good family name! Now I bear an even greater name than that given at my birth. It is a name given to me from the One whose name is above all names. With that new name He has set upon me, the title of a son, one who has been adopted into His family, honor above all honor and truth above all truth, I walk in this world gladly proclaiming His words. In Him I move and breathe and have my being. Mahalo, Yeshua!

Thank you to the Groomsman of all grooms!

Of all the men I've been welcomed by and of all I've welcomed, not one has exceeded in meaning or desire to me, than that of my son, my greatest gift, my unexpected one, my reward and my legacy. In him is the fullness of the groomsman who was never the groom. In him resides all I ever was, am, will be, and am not. It is the grooming of Reno-Oner that sets my soul at ease, and one day will close my eyes in peace and cause my heart to beat eternally and endlessly in him. He will fulfill my legacy worthy of its day, the gift of his earthly and Heavenly Father and the fulfillment of his visions and his father's dreams... Groom my son, groom on and be the groom and the groomsman. Help man, glorify G-d.

For My son the exquisite one!

The Beginning!

Pop (Always a groomsman and never the groom.)

Made in the USA
Lexington, KY
07 April 2012